When It's Football Time In Tennessee®

A Celebration of Tennessee's Football Traditions!

by Mark Stoudenmire

Cover and Chorus Art by Charlie Daniel

Illustrated by Michael Kane and R. Daniel Proctor

Vocal by Joel Reese

Steadman-Beiers Publishing, Inc., Knoxville, Tennessee

© 2007, Steadman-Beiers Publishing, Inc.

No part of this book may be reproduced or transmitted in any form or by any means, electronic or mechanical, including photocopying, recording, or by any information storage and retrieval system without written permission from the publisher.

Book designed by Lisa Bingham and Roger Greene, The Bingham Group, Knoxville, Tennessee.

Audio recording of "When It's Football Time in Tennessee" produced by Bryan Cumming at Studio 23, Nashville, Tennessee, and mastered by Larry Repasky at Christec Media, Nashville, Tennessee.

Audio cuts of Bobby Denton, John Ward, and Bob Kesling, which are inserted into "When It's Football Time in Tennessee," courtesy of Bobby Denton, Host Communications, Inc. / The Vol Network™, and The University of Tennessee®.

Audio recordings of The University of Tennessee "Pride of the Southland Band" courtesy of The University of Tennessee Bands and The University of Tennessee®.

The following words and phrases are registered trademarks of The University of Tennessee, Knoxville™ and are used herein by permission: University of Tennessee®; The University of Tennessee, Knoxville™; Tennessee®; Volunteers®; Tennessee Volunteers®; Vols®; Go Vols™; Big Orange™.

The phrase "The Vol Network™" is a registered trademark of Host Communications, Inc. and is used herein by permission.

Printed in Clarksville, Tennessee, U.S.A. by Jostens, Inc.

CD manufacturing by We Make Tapes & Discs, Nashville, Tennessee.

Library of Congress Control Number: 2005909176

ISBN 0-9774620-0-5

10 9 8 7 6 5 4 3 2 1

Published By:
Steadman-Beiers Publishing, Inc.
P.O. Box 51613
Knoxville, Tennessee 37950-1613

Dedication

This song and book are dedicated
to all those individuals
who work tirelessly in myriad capacities
to make the
Tennessee Volunteer Football experience

One of the Greatest!

and to
Tennessee Volunteer Fans, wherever you may be!

Verse 1

When it's Autumn time
in Tennessee,
the fields are rusty red;

The cornstalks blow
and the pumpkins glow
as the Sun bows down its head;

Verse 1

I long to be 'neath
the Maple trees,
their flaming hues ablaze;

To be back home
in Knoxville town,
so wondrous in many ways.

Verse 2

Old U.T.'s the place to be
on a clear, crisp,
Autumn Saturday;

When its kin
from the S.E.C. roll in
for a football game to play;

Verse 2

In Neyland Stadium's
bright array,
Orange from end to end,

The Tennessee Vols
in Orange and White
will stand the test again.

Verse 3

The Vols take a walk
down Peyton's Pass
just hours before the game,

As a pep band rings out
loud and clear
with spirit for those who came;

Verse 3

To cheer our men
of the gridiron on
as they march to battle royal;

The visiting team
with its glory dream
will soon be Old Smokey's foil.

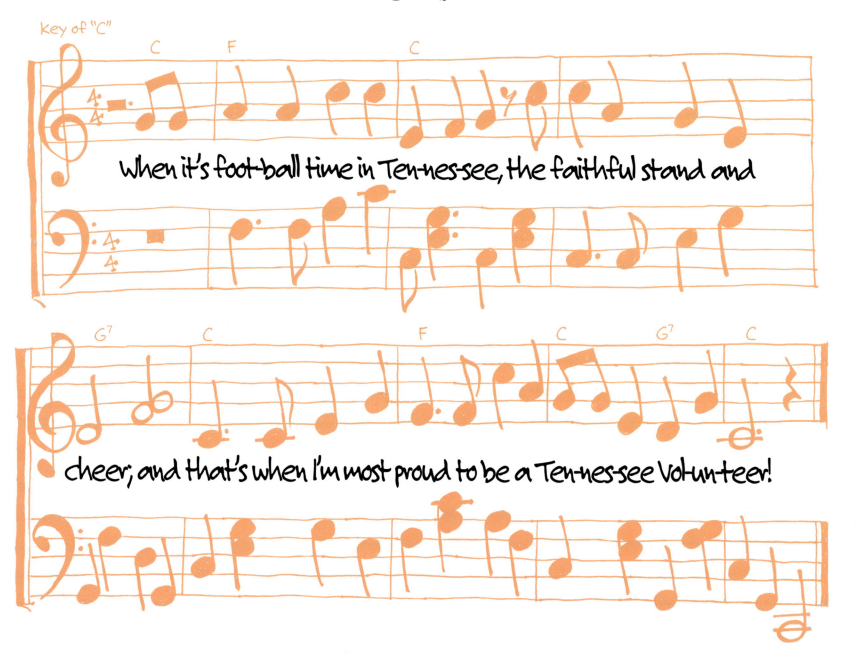

Verse 4

The "Pride of the Southland"
marches on
down Volunteer Boulevard;

Stadium-bound,
"Rocky Top" resounds
as they play out strong and hard;

Verse 4

As thousands clap, cheer and shout,
Neyland comes in view;

The Color and Pageantry of
Tennessee Football
shown in "Big Orange" hue!

Verse 5

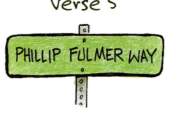

At Andy Holt Avenue and
Phillip Fulmer Way
"The Pride" gives all a thrill,

As hundreds peer
from the bridge above
and hundreds from "The Hill";

Verse 5

To the spirited sounds of
"Tennessee Waltz,"
"Rocky Top" and "Fight, Vols, Fight,"

The Majorettes whirl,
swirl and twirl
batons high to the crowd's delight.

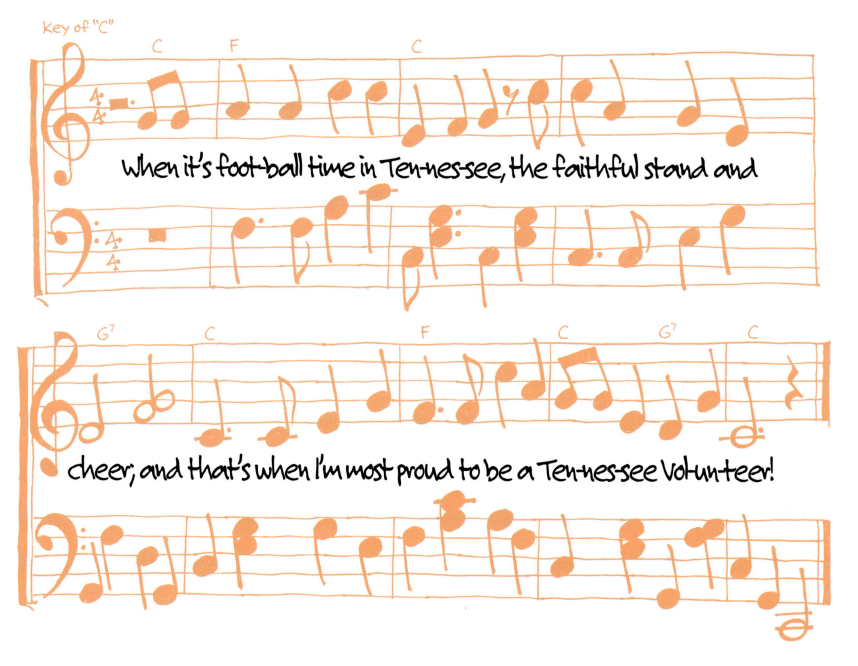

Verse 6

When a deep voice booms
a familiar croon
from the stadium's huge P.A.,

The faithful know
that football time's
not very far away;

Verse 6

But wha-da-ya pay for
"A Dog and a Coke®?"
Now the answer's in Tennessee lore;

Bobby Denton tells us:
"Pay These Prices
And Please Pay... No More!"

Verse 7

As the band marches
up and down the field,
the crowds join in the fray;

Cheers go 'round
to the rousing sound
of the "Pow'r T" on its way,

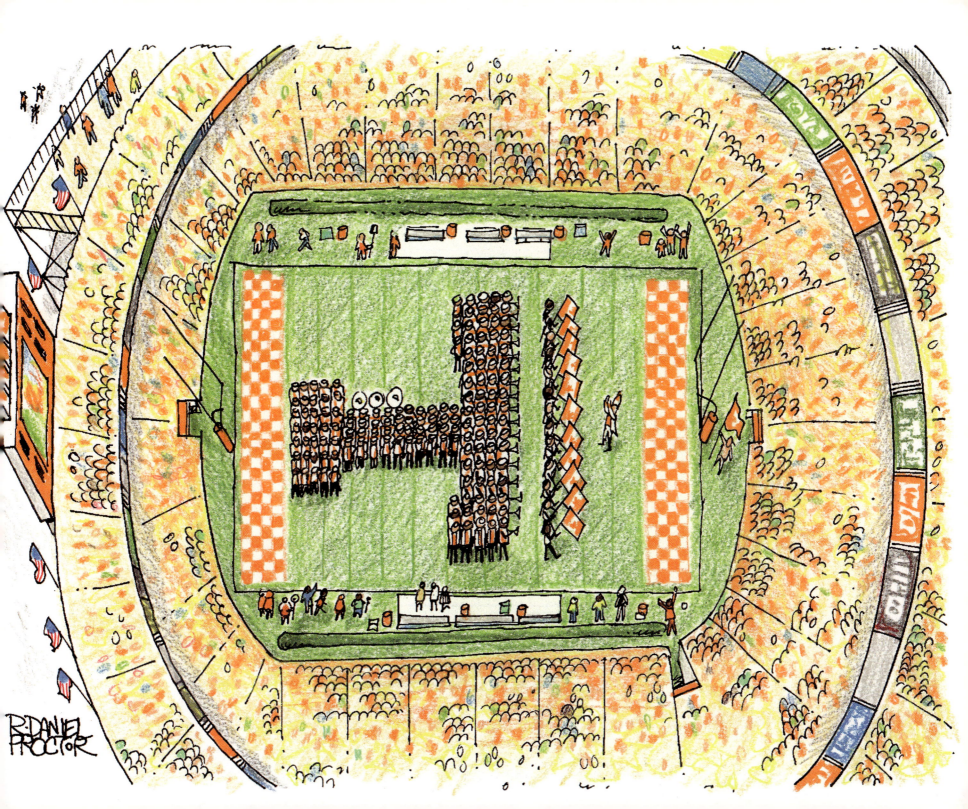

Verse 7

To the north end
of the stadium,
the "Giant T" to build;

You know "It's Football Time in Tennessee"
when through it
the Vols take the field.

Verse 8

Year after year
John Ward said the words
we all so loved to hear:

"It's Football Time in Tennessee,"
and fans 'round the world
would cheer;

Verse 8

Though the Vols
may be on the T.V. set,
a visual treat for all,

Radio would give us John's
and his sidekick
Bill Anderson's great call!

Verse 9

When thirty years expired,
John Ward retired
from Vol Network's game day cast;

But that's okay
'cause they found a way
to make his tradition last;

Verse 9

Bob Kesling's now
at the Radio's mike
for those Magical Moments neat;

As the kickoff flies
he, too, outcries
Those Five Magic Words So Sweet.

Verse 10

Our Conference foes
go down in woes
on Shields-Watkins Field;

The fans let fly
with a joyous cry
as victory is sealed;

Verse 10

The celebration's
long and sweet,
in to the evening hours;

Again we're blessed
with one of the nation's
strongest football powers!

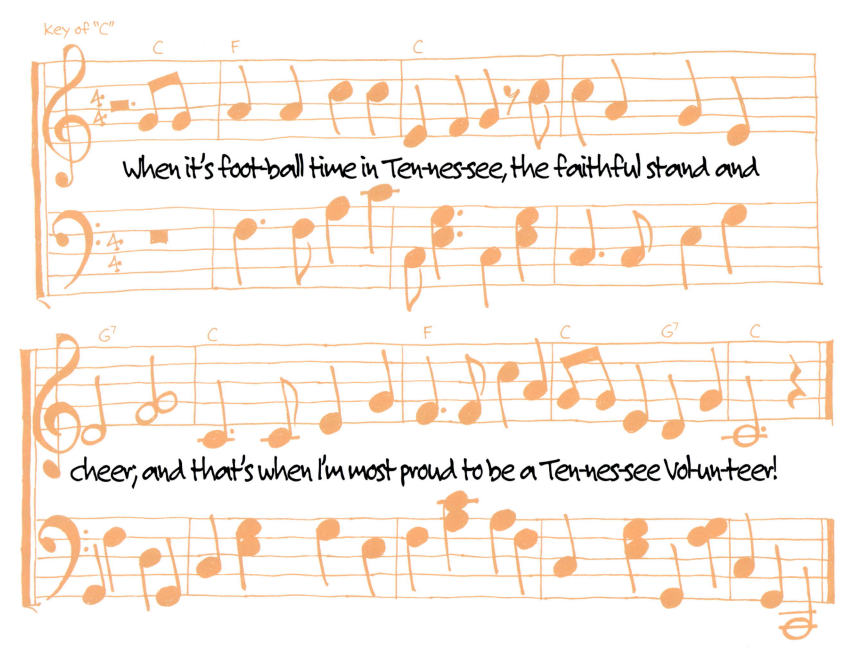

Content Outline

Verse 1:
Setting the Scene
"When It's Autumn Time in Tennessee"

Verse 2:
"Old U.T."
The University of Tennessee, Knoxville™

Verse 3:
"The Vol Walk"
Down "Peyton Manning Pass"

Chorus:
"When It's Football Time in Tennessee"

Verse 4:
"The Pride of the Southland Band"
Passing by "The Torchbearer"
The March to Neyland Stadium

Verse 5:
"Salute to the Hill"
At Andy Holt Avenue and Phillip Fulmer Way

Verse 6:
"Pay These Prices and Please Pay No More"
Bobby Denton, Stadium Public Address Play-by-Play Announcer since 1967

Verse 7:

The Pregame "T" Traditions
The "Power T"
The Vols Run Through the "T"

Verse 8:

"It's Football Time in Tennessee"
John Ward, "Voice of the Vols" Emeritus, Football Play-by-Play Announcer on Radio
from September 14, 1968 through January 4, 1999

Bill Anderson, Football Color Analyst on Radio
from September 14, 1968 through January 4, 1999

Verse 9:

"It's Football Time in Tennessee"
Bob Kesling, "Voice of the Vols," Football Play-by-Play Announcer on Radio since September 4, 1999

Tim Priest, Football Color Analyst on Radio since September 4, 1999

Jeff Francis, Football Sideline Reporter on Radio since September 4, 1999

Verse 10:

Shields-Watkins Field
Victory is Sealed!
The Celebration!

Personal Dedications

To Julie and the Kids, for encouraging this endeavor so totally; and
To Mom and my other Dad, Bev; and to Mrs. H. and all of our extended families; and
To the memory of Dad, Gerald, and Mr. H.
— *Mark Stoudenmire*

To my sweet wife Holly.
— *Bryan Cumming*

To Mark and his family for the belief in the creative dream; and
To Bryan and Holly for bringing such talented people together.
— *Joel Reese*

To Patsy – The Ink in My Well.
— *Charlie Daniel*

To Vickie, Jason, Adam & Amanda, Matthew, Bethany, Anna, Nathan, and Andrew;
What a great family!
— *Michael Kane*

To my girls: Nan, Ruthie and Becca.
— *R. Daniel Proctor*

Thanks to Mark and all of our wonderful clients who allow us to use the talents that God gave us.
— *The Bingham Group*

Acknowledgements

First and foremost, I thank God for all that worked together to bring to fruition this book and the recordings with which it is accompanied!

Next, the Heart and Soul of Tennessee Football! The student athletes, student performers and other student participants, the coaches, directors, teachers and instructors, the administrators, broadcasters, concessionaires, and everyone else who works or has worked long and hard in many different capacities to bring to us the pageantry and thrill of Tennessee football now and back across the years!

I also sincerely thank all of the following who assisted creatively and through their encouragement and help in the fulfillment of this endeavor:

Editorial Help and Suggestions: Leslie and Kevin Baggott; Kathy Burnett and her family; Charlie Daniel; David Lauver; the members of The Knoxville Songwriters' Association; my wife Julie and children Ken, Victoria, Elizabeth, and son-in-law Vadas Gintautas.

Vocals and Musical Direction: Bryan Cumming (producer, recording engineer, horn arrangements, background vocals, lyrical and musical suggestions); Joel Reese (lead vocalist, lyrical and musical suggestions); Julie Stoudenmire (background vocals, lyrical and musical suggestions); Larry Repasky of Christec Media in Nashville, Tennessee (mastering of "When It's Football Time in Tennessee").

The Musicians for "When It's Football Time in Tennessee" (Track 1 on the enclosed CD): Peck Horne (trombone, bass trumpet, tuba); Don Wayne (drums, clarinet, flute, piccolo); Ken Stoudenmire (trumpet, French horn, whistle). Peck and Ken are former members of the "Pride of the Southland Band."

The Illustrators: Charlie Daniel, of the Knoxville News Sentinel; Michael Kane, of His Light Studios; and R. Daniel Proctor, of the Knoxville News Sentinel.

Book Design and Production: Lisa Bingham, President, and Roger Greene, Production Manager, and the staff at The Bingham Group, Knoxville, Tennessee.

Licensing Assistance: Michael Young, Coordinator of Trademark Licensing for The University of Tennessee®, who directed us to The Collegiate Licensing Company (CLC), in Atlanta, Georgia, and graciously helped us along the way. Mr. Young assisted in the licensing process by providing much advice and counsel and by reviewing the art and music as they became available to keep us on the right track and expedite the receipt of approvals for the various aspects of the project.

Annie Weed, Senior Manager, Local/Restricted Licensing; Alli Stuetzer, Coordinator, Local/Restricted Licensing; and Noelle Sandhagen, Coordinator, Local/Restricted Licensing; all of CLC, who guided us and patiently waited while we worked through the licensing process.

The Audio Cuts: Glenn Thackston, Assistant General Manager / Director of Network Operations for Host Communications, Inc. / The Vol Network™, who obtained and granted approvals for our use of and then provided the audio cuts of Bobby Denton, John Ward, and Bob Kesling, which are incorporated into "When It's Football Time in Tennessee." Mr. Thackston graciously served as liaison in obtaining approvals from Mr. Denton, Mr. Ward, and Mr. Kesling for our use of their voices on the recording and their images in the illustrations and in obtaining approvals from Messrs. Bill Anderson, Tim Priest, and Jeff Francis for our use of their images in the illustrations.

Bobby Denton, John Ward, and Bob Kesling: for allowing us to use their voices on the recording and their images in the illustrations.
Bill Anderson, Tim Priest, and Jeff Francis: for allowing us to use their images in the illustrations.

The University of Tennessee "Pride of the Southland Band": Judy Dooley, Assistant to the Director of Bands: for handling our correspondence and assisting us in obtaining approval to include the U.T. Band's tracks on the CD; Dr. Gary Sousa, Director of Bands: for approving our use of the Band's tracks; Dr. Donald Ryder, Associate Director of Bands: for assisting us in obtaining approval and for providing the recordings of the U.T. Band that were included on the CD.

Use of the Music: Susan Jenkins at House of Bryant Publications: for approval of our use of "Rocky Top," written by Boudleaux and Felice Bryant. Ms. Jenkins also directed us to the proper agency to provide licensing for use of all the music.

Mark Stoudenmire
2007

For more information on the great traditions of Tennessee Volunteers® athletics, please visit

www.utsports.com

on the World Wide Web, and click on "Traditions" and "Vol Network™" in "Fan Zone"
on the left-hand side of the page.

Steadman-Beiers
PUBLISHING, INC.

From all of us who had a hand in producing *When It's Football Time in Tennessee,* we thank you for your interest in and purchase of our book. It is intended to be a tribute to the great traditions associated with Tennessee® football, and we sincerely hope that you enjoy it as such, and that you will visit The University of Tennessee® to experience these and other great traditions of Tennessee athletics firsthand.

For more information on *When It's Football Time in Tennessee,*
or to order additional copies of the book, please visit

www.whenitsfootballtimeintennessee.com

on the World Wide Web.

The Audio Recordings on Compact Disc (CD)

Track 1:

"When It's Football Time in Tennessee" – performed by Joel Reese (5:30)
Written by Mark Stoudenmire (Steadman-Beiers Publishing, Inc.)
Produced and recorded by Bryan Cumming at Studio 23, Nashville, Tennessee
Mastered by Larry Repasky at Christec Media, Nashville, Tennessee

The audio highlights of Bobby Denton, John Ward, and Bob Kesling
inserted into "When It's Football Time in Tennessee" are used by
permission and courtesy of Bobby Denton, Host Communications, Inc. /
The Vol Network™, and The University of Tennessee®.

Track 2:

"Rocky Top" (with singing) – performed by The University of Tennessee® "Pride of the Southland Band" (0:55)
Written by Boudleaux and Felice Bryant (House of Bryant Publications)

Track 3:

"Salute to the Hill" - performed by The University of Tennessee® "Pride of the Southland Band" (2:58)
Drum Intro
"Tennessee Waltz March" – written by Pee Wee King and Redd Stewart
(Sony/ATV Acuff Rose Music)
"Rocky Top" - Written by Boudleaux and Felice Bryant (House of Bryant Publications)
"Fight, Vols, Fight" – Written by Thornton W. Allen (Bro 'n Sis Music, Inc.)
Drum Outro